D1564508

GLUTEN SAFE & UNSAFE INGREDIENT LIST

THE FUNDAMENTAL POCKET GUIDE FOR CELIACS

Also by Jaqui Karr:

"Solace from depression"

A book that is a place of solace, support, understanding, and compassion - balanced with nutritional information that is relevant and immediately applicable. Besides the difficulties of life in general, our environment can make us truly ill or weaken our system to a point that makes it a challenge to cope. Learn how your health can be immediately improved. You can't beat something that you don't understand. Learn how to nourish your body properly and naturally so that you can give yourself the strength and physiological advantage to win.

"Gratitude is the Answer; the Secret to Happiness"

We have all had journals throughout the years, but it seems we write in them only when we are feeling good and have good things to write. In reality, we need inspiration more during times that we aren't feeling so great. This one is designed to help you through those challenging days, the days that you need a little help in changing your mood and mind frame. The author has shared parts of her own journal with you in the hope that perhaps a thought or a single word will help connect you to something you have become disconnected from, perhaps discover joy and pleasure from something you never noticed before. A unique journal that offers you the little nudge you might need to open your heart and mind to a place of serenity, beauty, gratitude...freedom...

Available from Amazon.com and other fine retailers worldwide

"This book is a must-have for anyone living with Celiac Disease. It contains a wealth of extremely valuable information, unknown to most health care practitioners. This book is filled with tips and tricks that can help patients avoid a great deal of pain and suffering. It is also a useful gift for friends and family of Celiac sufferers as it can help them understand the complexity and repercussions of the disease."

Dr. A. Lepage-Chaumont, N.D.
Pure Med Naturopathic Centre

NO
TWO
CELIACS

ARE EXACTLY THE SAME

Being a certified nutritionist, natural health consultant, as well as a Celiac myself, I have created this reference book to provide a practical on-hand guide to help manage a gluten free diet.

This guide provides the most complete and accurate list of safe and unsafe ingredients found in commercial products, where to look for hidden dangers, and why some common ingredients shown as safe on many gluten free lists are not necessarily always safe. You will also find several items that you will not see on most other lists, and crucial processing and packaging information that affect the safety of things we consume daily.

As a health consultant, I felt it important to also point out certain products - even though gluten free, that have been proven as toxic, yet are still legal. These have been indicated for your consideration.

This book is listed by ingredient, not final product, so that it is always current and relevant to you, regardless of geographic location, as well as when manufacturers change an ingredient (which is often). The advantage to you is to have a resource that is constant, a reliable reference that will always help you choose the right foods.

The slim, pocketbook format makes it easy to keep on hand and makes it convenient to carry with you when grocery shopping or traveling. Also, additional space is included to add items based on your individual reaction to specific foods or beverages.

The reality is that NO TWO CELIACS ARE ALIKE – this might be the most significant thing for any Celiac to remember. It means that besides the basic list of foods we all know we definitely cannot eat, there will be varied reactions to many other food items. Due to that fact, this list, or any other, can *never* be absolute.

It is important that you add your own list of what does not agree with your body. There are several blank pages at the back of this guide for you to keep track of any foods that don't work well with you. This will help you customize and keep this crucially important list all in one place, and keep you safe.

Please read the entire front section thoroughly – it is written in a concise, summarized way to make it easy to read quickly and it truly *is* ESSENTIAL information, including a specific vitamin and mineral list for Celiacs, particularly when newly diagnosed.

Managing a condition that imposes limitations on so many foods can be challenging, but like anything new, being well informed and having the proper tools makes all the difference.

I trust you will find this guide to be an invaluable tool and hope some words of encouragement from one Celiac to another provides you some comfort. In time, you will see that being a Celiac is actually quite a blessing; it provides wholesome eating habits, which in turn provides for much greater health.

I wish you infinite health and wellness.

Jaqui Karr, C.S.N.

NakedFood.ca

CONTENTS

ESSENTIAL BASICS - 11
A brief but important read

ESSENTIAL VITAMINS - 18

GRAINS & GLUTEN - 24

SAFE/UNSAFE INGREDIENTS - 26
☑safe   ⊗unsafe   **?** caution or specifics needed

NOTES - 60
For you to keep track of foods specific to your particular reactions

INDEX - 77
Page reference to specific topics covered in the Essential Basics section

ESSENTIAL BASICS

ARTIFICIAL FLAVOR/COLOR: always side with caution when you see vague or general terms. Food coloring can contain many ingredients within itself. Artificial flavors and colors may or may not be safe; only the manufacturer can confirm if they used any ingredients containing gluten.

CANDY, CHOCOLATE, COUGH DROPS: almost always dusted with flour to prevent sticking, and since the flour is not an actual ingredient IN the candy, the manufacturer usually will not list it. Today there are so many gluten free versions of these products available, it is quite easy to substitute. Look for specific labeling indicating gluten free.

CHEESE: most cheeses are safe, but not all. Blue cheese, Chilton, Roquefort are not safe; avoid veined cheeses or any that are coated with "mystery" products. Mystery products almost always contain gluten. Also avoid pre-shredded cheeses; they can be dusted with flour to prevent sticking. As with anything else you consume, check each ingredient on the label since recipes can vary.

COLAS & COMMON DRINKS: many of them are gluten free but caution with caramel coloring, it is an ingredient made up of several others, and the recipes vary. Be on alert with root beers, and any specially flavored drinks – the honey colored drinks should raise a flag. Distilled alcohol is generally safe, though vodka & rum manufacturers outright state their flavored vodkas are not safe for Celiacs. Wine coolers and regular beer are definitely unsafe, but there are GF versions available. Wine is safe (both red and white), as are champagne, port, and sherry.

11

CROSS-CONTAMINATION

Eating at a friend's or even hosting your own party, some simple precautions will go a long way. Double dipping can be a catastrophe. Ask your host to put aside a little plate with a spoon or two of dips before any guests arrive – this will ensure that no one with regular crackers or chips will contaminate food that you might also consume. Same rule applies to cheese; cut a few pieces of safe cheeses for yourself before substances from unsafe cheeses contaminate through the knives or platter. Avoid touching the bread basket when it is passed around – the flour dust can transfer easily to your hands. And please don't ever feel bad - you would happily accommodate anyone with a food intolerance and your friends will feel the same way.

When dining out, good humor and asking politely will certainly go a long way, but be sure you are clear about the severity of your gluten intolerance. Your health is ultimately your responsibility. Let's take a safe item like potatoes – if you are ordering fries, find out if other items, like breaded onion rings, are cooked in the same fryer. If so, then the oil will be contaminated. Whether eating out or at a friend's, never be shy to ask questions about preparation, seasoning, cooking tools. Consider things like gravy (usually thickened with flour). Take time to consider typical toppings or side dishes that may make an otherwise safe dish, unsafe.

For store bought foods, check every ingredient and when in doubt, contact the manufacturer. This is particularly important with ingredients that can be made from several sources, like maltodextrin. Also be cautious with ingredients within ingredients like vinegar in mayonnaise: the particular vinegar the manufacturer used may or may not be safe.

DETOX & DIETS: please proceed with caution and consult with your doctor. Any kind of diet, especially a restrictive one such as a diet with no fruit allowed, can create nutritional deficiencies (which is true for *any*one, Celiac or not). Good health comes from plenty of wholesome foods of a wide variety.

If you absolutely feel the need for a cleanse, consult with a knowledgeable, certified professional to guide you through a juice fast that includes plenty of nutrients. Avoid colon cleanses within first year of diagnoses as this will wash away minerals from your body at a time when you need to be restoring them.

A word about nutritionists: as much as they might mean well, there are very few who understand Celiac well. Be sure that their certification does not misguide you. Celiac is complex and should never be compared to standard diets or allergies.

GLUTEN FREE AND WHEAT FREE ARE NOT THE SAME: gluten comes in many forms (page 24) – check individual ingredients. "Wheat free" alone is not safe.

GRAS (GENERALLY RECOGNIZED AS SAFE): caution with the term "harmless level of gluten". Gastroenterologists with extensive Celiac experience will tell you there is no such thing as a harmless level of gluten to a Celiac. The only prudent way to handle this disease is to remain 100% gluten free.

GROCERY GUIDES: can misguide you because manufacturers regularly change their ingredients. Numerous items that were safe at the time the guide was published might not be safe just months later. By law, labels must always be changed when ingredients change, so the only truly safe route is to always check every ingredient on every label.

GROUND SPICE: buy spices in their whole form and grind at home (this also tastes so much better). Inexpensive grinders make it so simple. Besides the fact that pre-ground spices comprise risks of cross contamination, you might also be consuming harmful toxins. I.e. many table salts are bleached for a brighter white color; this is done with a harmful chemical that goes unnoticed since we consume salt in small doses. Good salt options are pure Himalayan or gray sea salt, it may cost you an extra few dollars a year – this is such a nominal amount, yet the cumulative effect of several minor changes will be significant.

KITCHEN CARE:
Get two cutting boards and make sure they are different materials to avoid mix-ups or residual matter; glass for gluten free and wood for standard (wood tends to trap substance even after washed).

Keep the standard food, utensils, toaster, on bottom shelves to keep crumbs from falling onto gluten free shelves. Same for refrigerator and cupboards – dedicate the top shelves for gluten free items.

Do not wipe crumbs from counters with the same hand or tea towels that you might use to dry plates.

Use different colored containers to store gluten free food. Keep two sets of colors to avoid mix-ups.

Tape "GF" stickers onto peanut butter jars, butter, and all other foods prone to double dipping or spreading onto bread; dedicate one set to remain gluten free.

-Do not be discouraged, these are all things that need to be set up just once, soon they will be second nature for you and your family.

MEDICATION: our focus is usually on food alone, especially when newly diagnosed, but *EVERY* single thing we digest must be checked. Unfortunately, your doctor will usually not know which medication is gluten free – but pharmacists can find out for you.

MINDSET: no different from everything else in life, your attitude towards this whole adventure will make all the difference in the world. Notice the reference to it as an adventure and not anything restrictive. If you moved to a foreign country and did not have access to the foods you are used to, you would undoubtedly adjust and enjoy new tastes. This is an opportunity for you to discover new foods and great new recipes.

MODIFIED – *ANYTHING*: unless you are 100% certain it is pure corn starch, it is unsafe. The term "modified food" or "modified x product" is very vague and unsafe. "Modified" can mean anything.

NATURAL FLAVOR & COLOR: Do not let the word "natural" misguide you; *wheat is a natural product...* Always be careful with vague and general terms.

NON-FOOD ITEMS: Cosmetics (particularly lipstick, lip balm) chewing gum, breath mints, toothpaste, mouthwash, envelopes, stamps, (buy self-sealing); look at everything you will digest with a sharper eye, and when in doubt – avoid or replace it.

RAW: of course going raw will ensure absolute safety, but it is not easy or convenient for most people. Even if not a completely raw diet, try to go to raw forms with as much as possible: i.e. homemade pesto instead of from a jar. You can't imagine how much better homemade salad dressings taste, and most will keep for over a week.

SAFE FOODS: be aware of seasoning, coloring, flavoring, marinades. The obvious may be simple: "avoid breaded chicken". Watch for the not-so-obvious like wheat in ice cream, barley in sauces and dressings, malt in chocolate, wheat in soy sauce...check ALL the ingredients in everything you consume.

SUSHI: very high risk of cross contamination with breaded, fried, tempura foods. There is also a major health concern outside of gluten; it is best explained in the extraordinary documentary "The Cove". "Mercury Rising" in the special features section discusses concerns with sushi; *highly recommended* to view this movie for health as well as environmental concerns.

TEA: many contain unsafe flavoring products, check labels carefully. There is a risk of cross contamination during the packaging process since most tea producers offer varieties of flavors. Teas are also an item where vague terms such as "natural flavors" are found often. Whenever possible, buy whole leaf teas.

THE LAW: most countries' laws state that an ingredient does not have to be listed if the product contains less than 100 grams (amount varies) per kilo or less than a certain number ppm (parts per million). ANY amount of gluten, no matter how little, is harmful to a Celiac. Please look out for petitions you can sign to help groups trying to get the government to change these dangerous laws; consumers have a right to know exactly what is in any product they buy.

VINEGAR: apple cider, distilled, wine, balsamic are usually safe. White vinegar might not be; the manufacturer can use wheat, rye or barley in their process and non-distilled contains gluten. If you do not have clear information, avoid it. Very inexpensive white vinegar should raise an alert flag and be verified.

VITAMIN DEFICIENCIES: Deficiencies caused by all autoimmune disorders are a very severe matter and can cause numerous complications including fatigue, depression, and other physical issues. If you have a gastroenterologist who knows Celiac well, by all means, work closely with them. You may also want to consult with a nutritionist to evaluate your diet, help you with substitutions to suit your lifestyle, as well as provide insight with whether or not you are consuming enough nutrients or require supplements.

Please be sure to confirm if your nutritionist thoroughly understands gluten intolerance. Also depending on how long you went undiagnosed (average Celiac goes undiagnosed for 11 years), your system may be in a serious state of deficiency and you will require special supplementation until you have restored what is necessary (essentials on next page).

VITAMINS & SUPPLEMENTS: Many contain fillers, binders, coloring, and/or flavoring. Always check all ingredients as you do with food.

Take whatever you can find in liquid or lozenge form; these are assimilated into your body more easily.

Without a doubt take enteric coated superior probiotics daily. You want enteric coated because you want the live acidophilus cells to reach your intestines intact – when they are not enteric coated, over 90% of their potency is lost with the natural acids in your stomach.

IMPORTANT TO NOTE: Supplementing may be necessary at first to restore your health and balance - avoid using supplements as a lifelong replacement for a balanced healthy diet. Ideally you want to be getting all your nutrients from organic foods in your daily diet.

ESSENTIAL VITAMINS: the following 4 pages will list the essential vitamins you need and some guidance on determining dosages. Celiac is complex and can cause a lot of complications that you can completely prevent, and many you can reverse. Cross check this list with your diet: i.e. if you drink pure orange juice, eat kiwis or strawberries daily, you don't need vitamin C supplements. Note there are many more benefits than listed here, details summarized to our focus.

Vitamins A and E: heal & repair the intestinal tract. A: 600-800 micrograms/day.   E: 400-600 IU/day.

B Complex: energy and proper digestion. If it does not contain at least 100mcg of **B6** and **B12 each**, take them in addition to the B Complex.

Folic Acid (called folate when from food): needed for protein metabolism, memory, fights depression. Critically important for pregnant women. 1mg/day.

Calcium, Vitamin D, Magnesium: listed together because you can usually find them in one pill or bottle, and because you absorb them better when taken together. Celiacs are very commonly deficient in all 3 of these. Vitamin D tells your body to absorb calcium as well as helps fight depression; most of us are not absorbing D from the 15-20 minutes of direct sun we need daily and need to supplement. New studies are also showing D as a preventative vitamin to MS and so much more. Calcium is critical for bone strength (exercise also important for this). Take soluble versions for better absorption: calcium citrate, lactate, or gluconate (not carbonate). Magnesium is also essential for bone health, proper function of muscles & nerves, and helps your body absorb calcium. Calcium & magnesium together help maintain normal pH value in the body.

Vitamin C: 250mg/day. This will strengthen your immune system, decrease stress and blood pressure, and cause your body to secrete lower levels of cortisol (stress hormone). WARNING: vitamin C boosts absorption of iron, which your body can not eliminate from your system (when in excess). Never take iron supplements without professional guidance.

Vitamin K: most Celiacs show a deficiency of this vitamin, which can lead to blood clotting. A superior multi-vitamin should contain the 10mcg needed.

Potassium: third most abundant mineral in the body, and commonly a deficiency in Celiacs. Eat a kiwi, banana, or potato 4-5 times/week. Kiwi is a superfood for many vitamins, daily intake is recommended.

Omega 3 Fatty Acids: vital for brain and nerve function. DHA helps brain cells communicate with each other, restore chemical balance, and prevent nerve abnormalities. Taken with B6, B12, and folate – it is an essential anti-depressant formula. DHA is formed with the correct ratio of omega 3 and 6. Best sources are krill oil & fish oil; absolutely critical to verify that you are buying mercury/cadmium/lead free products. 1000-2000mg/day.

Flax Seed Oil: A super oil containing omega 3's, 6's and 9's, B vitamins, potassium, lecithin, magnesium, fiber, protein, zinc, and 100 times richer in lignin than most whole grains. Incredibly long list of benefits, some of which are to reduce risk of breast & colon cancer, lower cholesterol, prevent blood clots, increase your own body's energy production and muscle recovery, stimulates brown fat cells facilitating weight loss, improves liver function, and can even treat some cases of depression. Everyone, Celiac or not, should be taking a minimum of 1000mg/day.

DETERMINING DOSAGES: the key element regarding dosages is that one size never fits all. Every person needs a customized formula based on their individual needs, and those needs will keep changing with age, changes in diet, activity level, and variations in health status.

The RDA (recommended dietary allowances) found on most products is usually far too low. RDA's were created decades ago to keep people alive by preventing diseases like scurvy. They were not created to provide optimal health and certainly are not current to the needs we face today due to diminished nutritional value and increased toxic value of our foods and water.

Unless you have blood tests showing deficiencies with particular items, you will need to do a little experimenting to see what works for you (of course, best option always is to coordinate with a professional). If you are managing supplements on your own, first thing to know is the difference between water and fat soluble vitamins.

Water soluble means your body can easily excrete what it doesn't need through your urine and sweat, so you don't need to worry about taking too much (within reason of course, 40,000mg of anything is harmful). Fat soluble means your body stores excess amounts in fats through your bloodstream; really excessive amounts can become toxic, but it takes very high amounts to get there. It is always best to consult with a qualified health care provider.

WATER SOLUBLE: all B vitamins, including folic acid, and vitamin C

FAT SOLUBLE: vitamins A, D, E, K

If you do consume a little too much in fat soluble, long before it gets to any toxic or dangerous level, you will feel yourself getting a little tired and lethargic – this is your body telling you there is too much for it to process. The trick is to go ahead with water soluble vitamins, and then with the fat soluble ones, start with RDA's and then one by one, increase dosages in small increments and see how you feel. This will take several months to accomplish because you need to isolate each fat soluble vitamin for 2-3 weeks as you try different levels. You must do this one at a time so that you know exactly how you are reacting to each particular vitamin.

When you start this process, your body might be quite depleted of certain vitamins and you will need higher amounts before you can bring it back down. For example, you may need 3000 IU/day of vitamin D for months before your system has stored enough to be at optimal level. Once your body is stable with correct stores, 600-1000 IU/day is sufficient. Do not be afraid when incrementing in small amounts.

What can be harmful in excessive amounts are iron, zinc, copper...these are easy to identify – they are the metals. And you'll notice they are not in the "essential vitamins" listed in this book. It is not recommended and can be harmful to experiment with metals without the guidance of a physician.

With fish oils or omega fatty acids, make sure you are buying a brand certified free of chemicals and metals (mercury, cadmium, lead). The optimum is to find a brand that uses an independent lab to test purity.

If you are fighting depression, the key elements are folic acid, B vitamins, and omega-3's (DHA/EPA).

The Discrepancies

As information is flooded in from various sources, you may find a lot of conflicting data. Foods listed as unsafe on some lists will be listed as safe on others and it can be very frustrating. There are many reasons this happens, one of which is that Celiac is not a black and white condition. Another main issue is that our small world shares much of its food in imports and exports, but there is no standard as far as labeling or process.

Even products all scientists agree to be safe may not be because when researchers experiment in a contained laboratory, they find the product to be safe. The reality is, several of those products, like quinoa and buckwheat, are often contaminated because they are processed and packaged in plants that also process regular wheat. If you visit one of these facilities and see the flour dust everywhere (looks like a snow blizzard in Canada, employees are walking around in astronaut suits), it becomes clear why anything else processed in that plant will be contaminated. These items have been marked with comments to help you proceed with caution, look for 100% GF facilities.

Some foods, like maltodextrin, can be made from wheat, potato, corn, or other starches. Known instances of this have been indicated; for these items, the manufacturer must clarify which product it used.

As well, different countries use different ingredients for the same food. An example is MSG: in the U.S. it is usually made with corn, outside the U.S. it is made with wheat or soy. If the testing lab used a soy based product and listed it as safe, but you consume the wheat version...this is also where many gluten free food guides go wrong.

It is frustrating to see "confirm with manufacturer" when you are expecting a list to tell you what is safe or unsafe. The reality is, NO list can truthfully claim to provide accurate information on every item – it's simply not possible. At best, a list can confirm most items, and indicate caution for indeterminate ones.

Whenever you are in doubt or a food listed as safe still seems to affect you in a negative way, keep track of it in your personal notes and completely avoid the food. Discuss these items with your doctor, they might be able to make a connection to other allergies or factors common to Celiacs.

Many Celiacs tend to develop food allergies apart from their gluten intolerance, like lactose intolerance or nut allergies. If you are on a completely gluten free diet yet still feel pain or even discomfort, ask your doctor for food allergy tests. It seems quite unfair for further allergies to be a side effect when we are already restricted to so many foods – but the reality is there are such worse illnesses out there, let's be grateful that ours can be managed through diet alone.

Fortunately, there are more and more new gluten free products coming onto the market; just be careful as government GF standards are not absolute – this guide will help identify potential areas of danger.

Food intolerances are rising at an alarming rate and will continue to rise until consumer demands force manufacturers to stop adding toxins to all our foods. In time, with heightened awareness and consumer pressure, the food industry will be forced to respond.

All of this may feel quite overwhelming at first, but it is critical information that will help you manage your new diet. *You'll have a handle on this before you know it.*

GRAINS AND GLUTEN

There are a handful of studies going back more than 20 years showing Celiac patients reacting to rice and/or corn yet most government agencies and medical communities are accepting corn and rice as safe. Most communities, *but not all.*

I know many of us rely heavily on rice when we eliminate other glutens from our diets, so yet another restriction is not welcome news.

If you have been gluten free for more than 6 months and still not feeling quite back to 100%, even if it is not full blown symptoms, perhaps eliminating rice and corn for 1-6 months would be a good experiment. If you find yourself feeling completely fantastic after a while, then you will know for yourself. I have listed them as unsafe in this guide because there are conflicting reports and we can't say with complete certainty that they are safe. Perhaps there are variables that differ from one Celiac to another so while one may tolerate these grains well, another may not. Those variables are far from being discovered. Right now the focus is on methods of testing, looking for certain genes, etc.

As it stands, I don't think the medical community will be presenting a unanimous decision anytime soon, if ever, so it will remain up to each individual to make a choice. We don't know yet what the long term effects of continuous digestion of small amounts of gluten are and we know that in most cases the person will be suffering internal damage with no external symptoms.

This one will come down to individual decisions; sadly the burden sits with you, the patient.

The most controversial discrepancy: corn and rice are "known" as safe yet all grains have gluten. The reason some have been labeled as safe is due to the lower levels of gluten or lower levels of glutamine. "Prolamins" are: proteins high in PROLine and glutAMINe. Gliadin and glutenin are the prolamins for wheat, and this being the highest percentage of gluten within grains has become the focus of most studies, but gliadin is not the only offender to Celiac Disease.

Barley (hordein 45-55%)
Corn (zein 55%)
Millet (panicin 20-40%)*
Oats (avenin 16%)
Rice (orzenin 5%)
Rye (secalin 30-50%)
Sorgum (kafirin 52%)
Wheat (gliadin/glutenin 69%)

*Millet may be a controversy within a controversy – some studies claim it has zero gluten because its prolamin is not "glutelin-like", particularly in the finger & foxtail varieties. These are generally older studies and not considering Celiac.

We know some patients react to corn, rice, and all other grains, but we don't know why others might not. Issues to consider:

1) The body's immediate reaction, or lack thereof, (even with those who react acutely with higher levels of gluten) is not a good measuring stick
2) We don't yet know what the long term implications of small amounts (as in rice) of gluten are. Please read the article posted at: Naked.Food.ca/legal.php

Again, due to the conflicting studies, rice, corn, and their by-products have been marked as unsafe in this guide – but ultimately the decision is yours.

GLUTEN FREE VERSIONS OF MANY UNSAFE PRODUCTS, LIKE BEERS AND CERTAIN CHEESES, ARE NOW AVAILABLE – your motto should always be "check every ingredient on every label"

SAFE & UNSAFE INGREDIENT LIST

☑safe   ⊗unsafe   ? caution or specifics needed

⊗Abyssinian Hard (wheat triticum durum)
☑Acacia Gum
☑Acesulfame K
☑Acesulfame Potassium
☑Acetanisole
☑Acetic Acid
☑Acetic Anhydride
☑Acetolactate Decarboxylase
☑Acetone
☑Acetone Peroxide
☑Acetophenone
⊗Acidophilus Milk
☑Acorn Quercus
☑Active Bacterial Cultures
☑Adipic Acid
☑Adzuki Bean
☑Agar
☑Agave
☑Alant Starch
☑Albumen
? Alcohol:
    SAFE: Distilled alcohol [unflavored gin, rum, vodka, whiskey], champagne, port, sherry, wine.
    NOT SAFE: Specially flavored rum, vodka, premixes, beer, wine coolers. Sake contains Koji, which may contain barley. Cider may contain barley enzymes.
    As with food, if all the ingredients haven't been verified or are unavailable, refrain until you can verify with manufacturer or find a gluten free substitute

⊗Ale
☑Alfalfa
☑Algae
☑Algin
☑Alginate
☑Alginic Acid
☑Alkalized Cocoa
☑Alkanet
☑Allicin
☑Allura Red
☑Almond
☑Alpha-amylase
☑Alpha-lactalbumin
☑Alpha-tocopherol Acetate
☑Aluminum
☑Amaranth (possible cross contamination)
☑Ambergris
☑Ammonium Alginate
☑Ammonium Bicarbonate or Carbonate
☑Ammonium Carrageenan
☑Ammonium Chloride
☑Ammonium Citrate
☑Ammonium Furcelleran
☑Ammonium Hydroxide
☑Ammonium Persulphate
☑Ammonium Phosphate
☑Ammonium Sulphate
⊗Amp-Isostearoyl Hydrolyzed Wheat Protein
☑Amylase
☑Amylopectin
☑Amylose
☑Anise

☑Annatto
?Annatto Color (multiple processing methods)
☑Anthocyanins
☑Apple Cider Vinegar
☑Arabic Gum
☑Arabinogalactan
⊗Arborio Rice (see page 24)
☑Arrowroot (pure arrowroot is safe; commercially prepared arrow biscuits usually contain gluten)
?Artificial Butter Flavor (recipes/ingredients vary)
?Artificial Color (vague)
?Artificial Flavor (vague)
⊗Asafoetida (spice, often contains flour)
☑Ascorbic Acid
☑Aspartame (gluten free, but highly toxic)
☑Aspartic Acid
☑Aspic
☑Astragalus Gummifer
⊗Atta Flour
☑Autolyzed Yeast Extract
⊗Avena Sativa (oats - see page 24)
⊗Avenin (see page 24)
☑Avidin
☑Azodicarbonamide (gluten free, but toxic)
☑Bacon (caution flavoring/spices)
☑Bacterial Cultures
?Baking Powder (verify which starch is used)
?Baking Soda (verify all ingredients, not all are safe)
☑Balsamic Vinegar
⊗Barley
⊗Barley Grass
⊗Barley Hordeum Vulgare
⊗Barley Malt

⊗Basmati Rice (see page 24)
☑Beans
⊗Beer
☑Beeswax
☑Bengal Gram
☑Benzoic Acid
☑Benzoyl Peroxide
☑Benzyl Alcohol
☑Besan bean (chickpea)
☑Beta Carotene
⊗Beta Glucan (oats - see page 24)
☑Betaine
☑BHA
☑BHT
☑Bicarbonate of Soda
☑Biotin
⊗Black Rice (see page 24)
⊗Bleached Flour
⊗Blue Cheese (small amounts of flour in the mold)
⊗Bouillon
☑Bovine Rennet
⊗Bran
⊗Bread Flour
⊗Brewer's Rice (see page 24)
⊗Brewer's Yeast
⊗Brie Cheese (caution with coating)
☑Bromelain
☑Brominated Vegetable Oil (gluten free, often in colas, toxic in high amounts and banned in many countries)
⊗Broth (many GF versions available)
⊗Brown Flour

⊗ Brown Rice Syrup (see page 24)
☑ Brown Sugar
☑ Buckwheat (risk of cross contamination)
⊗ Bulgur
☑ Butter (unflavored, check ingredients)
? Buttermilk (most contain modified food starch)
⊗ Butterscotch
☑ Butylated Hydroxyanisole
☑ Butylated Hydroxytoluene
☑ Butyl Compounds
☑ Caffeine
☑ Calcium Acetate
☑ Calcium Alginate
☑ Calcium Aluminum Silicate
☑ Calcium Ascorbate
☑ Calcium Carbonate
☑ Calcium Carrageenan
? Calcium Caseinate (contains MSG)
☑ Calcium Chloride
☑ Calcium Citrate
☑ Calcium Disodium
☑ Calcium Fumarate
☑ Calcium Furcelleran
☑ Calcium Gluconate
☑ Calcium Glycerophosphate
☑ Calcium Hydroxide
☑ Calcium Hypophosphite
☑ Calcium Iodate
☑ Calcium Lactate
☑ Calcium Pantothenate
☑ Calcium Peroxide
☑ Calcium Phosphate

☑Calcium Propionate

☑Calcium Silicate

☑Calcium Sorbate

☑Calcium Stearate

☑Calcium Stearoyl Lactylate

☑Calcium Sulfate

☑Calcium Tartrate

⊗Calrose Rice (see page 24)

⊗Camembert Cheese (caution with coating)

☑Camphor (gluten free, poisonous in large amounts)

?Candy (often dusted with flour to prevent sticking)

☑Cane Sugar

☑Cane Vinegar

☑Canola Oil (also called rapeseed oil. made from the seed of rape - which is in the grass family. tested as safe but many Celiacs have adverse reactions. Canola is a genetically modified product that your body doesn't process well)

☑Canthaxanthin

☑Caprylic Acid

?Caramel Color (often made with barley malt, manufacturer must confirm ingredients used)

☑Caraway Seeds

☑Carbonated Water

☑Carbon Dioxide

☑Carboxymethyl Cellulose

☑Carmine

☑Carnauba Wax

☑Carob Bean

☑Carob Bean Gum

☑Carob Flour

☑Carrageenan

☑Carrageenan Chondrus Crispus

☑Casein
☑Cassava Manihot Esculenta
☑Castor Oil
☑Catalase
☑Cellulase
☑Cellulose
☑Cellulose Ether
☑Cellulose Gum
⊗Cereal Binding
☑Cetyl Alcohol
☑Cetyl Stearyl Alcohol
☑Champagne Vinegar
☑Channa (chickpea)
☑Charcoal
?Cheese (not all are safe, check the labels carefully; blue and veined cheese usually contain trace amounts of flour, also avoid pre-shredded cheeses as they are usually coated with flour to avoid sticking or clumping)
☑Chestnuts
☑Chia
☑Chicken (fresh is safe; caution with pre-seasoned)
☑Chickpea
⊗Chilton cheese
☑Chlorella
☑Chlorine
☑Chloropentafluoroethane
☑Chlorophyll
?Chocolate (usually unsafe, also many bars are dusted with flour to avoid sticking to wrapping)
?Chocolate Liquor (look for added ingredients)
☑Cholecalciferol
☑Choline Chloride

⊗Chorizo (usually contain cereal fillers, avoid if you don't have detailed label or verify with manufacturer)

⊗Chow Mein Noodles

☑Chromium Citrate

☑Chymosin

?Citric Acid (verify source used)

?Clarifying Agents (may be hydrolyzed wheat)

⊗Club Wheat (triticum aestivum subspecies compactum)

☑Cochineal

☑Cocoa (verify it is pure cocoa)

☑Cocoa Butter

☑Coconut

☑Coconut Flour

☑Coconut Oil

☑Coconut Vinegar

☑Coffee (pure coffee is safe, though many Celiacs are sensitive - careful with flavors added when buying lattes and cappuccinos, or flavored milk)

☑Collagen

☑Colloidal Silicon Dioxide

⊗Common Wheat (Triticum aestivum)

☑Confectioner's Glaze or Sugar

⊗Converted® Rice (see page 24)

?Cooking Spray (many contain grain or flour alcohol)

☑Copernicia Cerifera

☑Copper Sulphate

⊗Corn and all by-products (see page 24)

☑Cortisone

☑Cotton Seed

☑Cotton Seed Oil

⊗ Couscous
☑ Cowitch
☑ Cowpea
⊗ Cracker Meal
☑ Cream of Tartar (watch for added flavoring)
⊗ Criped Rice
☑ Crospovidone
⊗ Croutons
☑ Curcumin
☑ Curds
☑ Curry (pure curry safe; paste may contain gluten)
⊗ Custard
☑ Cyanocobalamin
☑ Cyclamate
☑ Cysteine, L
☑ Dal or Dahl (lentils)
☑ D-Alpha-tocopherol
☑ Dasheen Flour (taro)
☑ Dates (may be coated to prevent sticking)
☑ D-Calcium Pantothenate
☑ Delactosed Whey (pure whey safe; altered versions may contain gluten)
⊗ Della Rice (see page 24)
☑ Demineralized Whey (pure whey safe; altered versions may contain gluten)
☑ Desamidocollagen
☑ Dextran
? Dextrate (may be from any starch)
? Dextri-maltose (wheat barley may be used)
? Dextrin (can be made from wheat, corn, or several other grains; *supposed* to be indicated when wheat)
☑ Dextrose
☑ Dhal

☑Dhalin

☑Dichloromethane

☑Diglyceride (unmodified)

☑Dimethylpolysiloxane Formulations

⊗Dinkle (Spelt)

☑Dioctyl Sodium

☑Dioctyl Sodium Solfosuccinate

☑Dipotassium Phosphate

☑Disodium EDTA

☑Disodium Guanylate

☑Disodium Inosinate

☑Disodium Phosphate

⊗Disodium Wheatgermamido Peg-2 Sulfosuccinate

☑Distilled Alcohol (distillation process makes it safe; caution with added flavors, additives, color)

☑Distilled Vinegar (see "vinegar")

☑Dry Roasted Nuts (risk of cross contamination and seasoning)

⊗Durum Wheat (Triticum durum)

☑Dutch Processed Cocoa

?Edible Coatings/Films (may be corn or wheat)

⊗Edible Starch

☑EDTA (ethylenediaminetetraacetic acid)

☑Eggs

⊗Einkorn (Triticum monococcum)

☑Elastin

⊗Emmer (Triticum dicoccon)

⊗Emulsifiers (most contain gluten)

⊗Enriched Flour

⊗Enzymes (may contain binders)

☑Epichlorohydrin

☑Ergocalciferol

☑Erthorbic Acid

☑Erythritol
☑Erythrosine
☑Ester Gum
☑Ethanol
☑Ethoxyquin
☑Ethyl Alcohol
☑Ethylenediaminetetraacetic Acid
☑Ethyl Maltol
☑Ethyl Vanillin
☑Expeller Pressed Canola Oil (see Canola)
⊗Farina
⊗Farina Graham
⊗Farro
☑Fava Bean
☑Fennel
☑Ferric Orthophosphate
☑Ferrous Fumerate
☑Ferrous Gluconate
☑Ferrous Lactate
☑Ferrous Sulfate
☑Feta Cheese
⊗Filler (too vague, usually wheat)
☑Fish (caution with breaded, pre-seasoned, fried)
⊗Flaked Rice (see page 24)
?Flavoring (vague term)
☑Flax
⊗Flour (standard is wheat)
☑Flour Salt
☑Folacin
☑Folate
☑Folic Acid
?Food Coloring (vague)
?Food Starch (can be wheat or mixture)

☑Formaldehyde (gluten free, but toxic)
☑Fructose
☑Fructose Syrup (unflavored, for corn/corn fructose see page 24)
☑Fruit (if dried, verify for additives)
☑Fruit Juice Concentrate
☑Fruit Vinegar
⊗Fu (dried wheat gluten)
☑Fumaric Acid
☑Furcelleran
☑Galactose
?Gamma Oryzanol (verify starch used)
☑Garbanzo Beans
☑Garlic
☑Gelatin
?Gelatinized Starch (verify type of starch)
☑Gellan Gum
⊗Germ
⊗German Wheat
⊗Gliadin
☑Glucanase
☑Glucoamylase
☑Gluconic Acid
☑Glucono Lactone (Glucono-Delta)
☑Glucose
☑Glucose Isomerase
☑Glucose Oxidase
?Glucose Syrup (can be corn or wheat; usually listed as safe because the wheat forms are trace amounts. regardless of PPM level, *any* amount of gluten is not safe for a Celiac)
☑Glutamate

? Glutamic Acid (MSG, can be from several grains)
? Glutamine - glutamine & L-glutamine are the same: SAFE if the source is from animal protein or vegetable; UNSAFE when derived from wheat, peptide or bonded
⊗ Glutamine Peptide (usually derived from wheat)
⊗ Gluten
⊗ Glutenin
⊗ Gluten Peptides
⊗ Glutinous Rice   (see page 24)
? Glycerides (modified versions may contain wheat, unmodified are just fats and are safe)
☑ Glycerin
☑ Glycerol Diacetate
☑ Glycerol Monoacetate
☑ Glycerol Monooleate
☑ Glyceryl Triacetate
☑ Glyceryl Tributyrate
☑ Glycine
☑ Glycol
☑ Glycolic Acid
☑ Glycol Monosterate
⊗ Gorgonzola Cheese
⊗ Graham Flour
☑ Gram flour (chick peas)
⊗ Granary Flour (may be combination of grains)
☑ Grape Skin Extract
? Gravy (usually thickened with wheat flour, can be safe if pure corn starch)
⊗ Grits (corn – see page 24)
⊗ Groats (barley, wheat)
? Ground Spices (cross contamination/filler risk)
☑ Guaiaca Gum
☑ Guar Gum (guaran, can have IBS effect)
☑ Gum Acacia

☑Gum Arabic

?Gum Base (manufacturer must confirm source)

☑Gum Benzoin

☑Gum Guaiacum

☑Gum Tragacanth

⊗Hard Wheat

⊗Heeng

☑Hemicellulase

⊗Hemp (often listed as gluten free, but has been tested with 15 ppm gliadin)

☑Herbs (look for pure, many have fillers)

☑Herb Vinegar

☑Hexane

☑Hexanedioic Acid

⊗High Fructose Corn Syrup (see page 24)

⊗Hing

☑Hominy

☑Honey

☑Hops

⊗Hordein

⊗Hordeum Vulgare Extract

☑Horseradish (pure)

⊗HPP

?Hulls (outer layer of any grain)

⊗HVP

☑Hyacinth Bean

☑Hydrochloric Acid

⊗Hydrogenated Corn Starch

⊗Hydrogenated Starch Hydrolysate

☑Hydrogenated Vegetable Oil

☑Hydrogen Peroxide

☑Hydrolyzed Caseinate

☑Hydrolyzed Meat Protein

? Hydrolyzed Oat Protein (may contain wheat)
? Hydrolyzed Plant Protein (may contain wheat)
☑ Hydrolyzed Soy Protein
? Hydrolyzed Vegetable Protein (may contain wheat)
⊗ Hydrolyzed Wheat Gluten
⊗ Hydrolyzed Wheat Protein Pg-Propyl Silanetriol
⊗ Hydrolyzed Wheat Starch
☑ Hydroxylated Lecithin
☑ Hydroxypropyl Cellulose
☑ Hydroxypropyl Methylcellulose
⊗ Hydroxypropyltrimonium Hydrolyzed Wheat Protein
☑ Hypromellose
? Ice Cream (check ingredients, most have gluten)
⊗ Ice Cream Cones
☑ Illepe
☑ Indian Ricegrass seed (Montina)
☑ Indigotine
☑ Inulin
☑ Inulinase
☑ Invertase
☑ Invert Sugar
☑ Iodine
☑ Irish Moss Gelose
☑ Iron Ammonium Citrate
☑ Iron Oxide
☑ Isinglass
☑ Iso-Ascorbic Acid
☑ Isobutane
☑ Isolated Soy Protein
☑ Isomalt
☑ Isopropanol
☑ Isopropyl Alcohol
⊗ Japonica Rice (see page 24)

⊗Jasmine Rice (see page 24)

☑Job's Tears (Hato Mugi, Juno's Tears, River Grain)

⊗Jowar (Sorghum, see page 24)

⊗Kafirin

⊗Kamut (pasta wheat)

☑Karaya Gum

☑Kasha (Russian Kasha may contain millet and oats)

☑K-Carmine Color

⊗Kecap Manis (soy sauce)

☑Kelp

☑Keratin

☑Ketchup (check ingredients, many unsafe)

⊗Ketjap Manis (soy sauce)

☑K-Gelatin

⊗Kluski Pasta

?Koji (verify starch used)

☑Konjac

⊗Koshihikari (rice – see page 24)

☑Kudzu

☑Kudzu Root Starch

☑Lactalbumin Phosphate

☑Lactase

☑Lactic Acid

☑Lactitol

☑Lactobacillus Acidophilus

☑Lactobacillus Bifidus

⊗Lacto globulin

☑Lactose (many Celiacs intolerant; reaction generally improves after adhering to GF diet for some time)

☑Lactulose

☑Lactylic Esters of fatty acids

☑Lanolin

☑Lard
☑L-Cysteine
☑Lecithin (soy sensitive for some Celiacs)
☑Lecithin Citrate
☑Legumes
☑Lemon Grass
☑Lentils (careful with cross-contamination)
? L-Glutamine (see glutamine)
☑Licorice Candy or Extract (check with manufacturer)
☑Lipase
☑Lipoxidase
? Liquor (see alcohol)
☑L-Leucine
☑L-Lysine
☑L-Methionine
☑Locust Bean Gum
☑L-Tryptophan
☑Lysozyme
⊗Macha Wheat (triticum aestivum)
☑Magnesium Aluminum Silicate
☑Magnesium Carbonate
☑Magnesium Chloride
☑Magnesium Citrate
☑Magnesium Fumerate
☑Magnesium Hydroxide
☑Magnesium Oxide
☑Magnesium Phosphate
☑Magnesium Silicate
☑Magnesium Stearate
☑Magnesium Sulphate
⊗Maida (Indian wheat flour)
⊗Maize (corn – see page 24)

⊗ Maize Waxy

☑ Malic Acid

⊗ Malt

⊗ Malt Chocolate

⊗ Malted Barley Flour

⊗ Malted Milk

⊗ Malt Extract

⊗ Malt Flavoring

⊗ Maltitol (usually listed as safe because process is supposed to remove gluten from the wheat starch – trace amounts will always be left)

? Maltodextrin (can be made from wheat, potato, rice or corn. listed as safe on most GF lists because it is a highly processed product, so assumption is gluten is removed even with wheat versions, but trace amounts may be left on product; not safe unless potato)

☑ Maltol

⊗ Maltose (listed as safe on most lists because the manufacturing process is said to remove the gluten from end product; trace amounts or more may be left)

⊗ Malt Syrup

⊗ Malt Vinegar

☑ Manganese Sulfate

☑ Manioc

☑ Mannitol

☑ Maple Syrup (pure, unflavored)

☑ Margarine (check all ingredients)

⊗ Masa Farina (cornstarch)

⊗ Masa Flour

⊗ Masa Harina

⊗ Matza

⊗ Matzah

⊗ Matzo

⊗ Matzo Semolina

☑Meat (watch for fillers, flavoring)
☑Medium Chain Triglycerides
☑Menhaden Oil
⊗Meringue
⊗Meripro 711
☑Methanol
☑Methyl Alcohol
☑Methyl Cellulose
☑Methyl Paraben
☑Microcrystalline Cellulose
☑Micro-Particulated Egg White Protein
☑Milk (technically safe, but many Celiacs sensitive –
see "lactose". Caution if flavored; malted milk not safe)
☑Milk Protein Isolate (see milk or lactose)
⊗Millet (see page 24)
⊗Milo (Sorghum)
☑Mineral Oil
☑Mineral Salts
⊗Mir
⊗Mirin (many brands contain wheat)
⊗Miso
⊗Modified Corn Starch (see page 24)
?Modified Food Starch (caution, vague term)
☑Molasses (unflavored)
☑Molybdenum Amino Acid Chelate
☑Monoacetin (gluten free, food additive, also used as
gelatinizing agent in explosives and leather tanning)
☑Monocalcium Phosphate
☑Monoglyceride (unmodified)
☑Monoisopropyl Citrate
☑Monopotassium Phosphate
☑Monosaccharides

? Monosodium Glutamate (see MSG)

☑Monostearates

? MSG (can be made from seaweed, wheat, or corn; always side with caution)

☑Mung Bean

☑Musk

☑Mustard powder or sauce (verify all ingredients)

☑Myristic Acid

☑Natamycin

? Natural Flavors (vague)

? Natural Juices (vague)

☑Natural Smoke Flavor

☑Neotame (gluten free, but toxic)

☑Niacin

☑Niacinamide

⊗Nishasta

☑Nitrates

☑Nitric Acid

☑Nitrogen

☑Nitrous Oxide

☑Non-fat Milk (unflavored, check additives)

☑Nori

☑Nuts (watch for risk of cross contamination in the roasting process and seasonings)

⊗Oat, Oatmeal, Oatrim (see page 24)

☑Oleic Acid

☑Oleoresin

☑Olestra (brand name Olean, gluten free, but a very harmful product found in many potato chips)

☑Oleyl Alcohol/Oil

☑Olive Oil

☑Orange B

☑Orchil

⊗Oriental Wheat (triticum turanicum)
⊗Oryzanol (usually rice bran oil, corn or barley)
⊗Orzenin (see page 24)
⊗Orzo Pasta
☑Oxystearin
☑Ozone
☑Palmitate
☑Palmitic Acid
☑Palm Kernel Oil (gluten free, but coconut oil is more environmentally friendly)
⊗Panicin (see page 24)
☑Pancreatin
☑Pantothenic Acid
☑Papain
☑Paprika
☑Paraffin
⊗Pasta (standard is wheat)
☑Pea - Chick
☑Pea - Cow
☑Pea Flour
☑Peanut (caution with roasted or seasoned)
☑Peanut Flour
☑Peanut Oil
⊗Pearl Barley
⊗Pearl Rice
☑Peas
☑Pea Starch
☑Pectin
☑Pectinase
☑Pentosanase
☑Peppermint Oil

☑Peppers
☑Pepsin
⊗Peptide Bonded Glutamine (usually wheat)
☑Peracetic Acid
⊗Persian Wheat (triticum carthlicum)
☑Peru Balsam
⊗Perungayam
☑Petrolatum
☑PGPR (Polyglycerol Polyricinoleate)
☑Phenylalanine
☑Phosphate (Calcium)
☑Phosphoric Acid
☑Phosphoric Glycol
☑Phosphorus Oxychloride
☑Pigeon Peas
☑Poi
⊗Polenta (corn – see page 24)
⊗Polished Rice
⊗Polish Wheat (triticum polonicum)
☑Polydextrose
☑Polyethylene Glycol
☑Polyglycerol
☑Polyglycerol Polyricinoleate (PGPR)
☑Polysorbates
⊗Popcorn (see page 24)
⊗Popcorn Rice (see page 24)
⊗Porter
☑Potassium Acid Tartrate
☑Potassium Benzoate
☑Potassium Bicarbonate
☑Potassium Bisulphite
☑Potassium Carbonate

☑Potassium Carrageenan
☑Potassium Caseinate
☑Potassium Citrate
☑Potassium Fumarate
☑Potassium Furcelleran
☑Potassium Hydroxide
☑Potassium Iodate
☑Potassium Iodide
☑Potassium Lactate
☑Potassium Matabisulphite
☑Potassium Nitrate
☑Potassium Phosphate
☑Potassium Sorbate
☑Potassium Stearate
☑Potassium Sulphate
☑Potassium Tartrate
☑Potato
?Potato Chips (look for specific GF products; usually unsafe due to seasonings and processing methods)
☑Potato Flour
☑Potato Starch
⊗Poulard Wheat (triticum turgidum)
☑Povidone
?Powdered Sugar (may contain gluten)
?Pregelatinized Starch (may be from any starch)
⊗Pretzels (many GF varieties available)
☑Prinus
☑Pristane
⊗Prolamin (see page 24)
☑Propionic Acid
☑Propolis
☑Propylene Glycol
☑Propylene Glycol Monosterate

☑Propyl Gallate
☑Protease
⊗Protein Hydrolysates
☑Psyllium
☑Pullulanase
☑Pyridoxine Hydrochloride
☑Pyrophosphate
☑Quinoa (risk of cross-contamination)
⊗Ragi (also called finger or African millet)
☑Raisin Vinegar
☑Rape (see Canola)
☑Recaldent
⊗Red Rice (see page 24)
☑Reduced Iron
☑Rennet
☑Rennet Casein
☑Resinous Glaze
☑Reticulin
☑Riboflavin
⊗Rice (see page 24)
⊗Rice Bran
⊗Rice Bran Oil
⊗Rice Flour
⊗Rice Malt (can also contain barley or Koji)
⊗Rice Milk
⊗Rice Paper
⊗Rice Polishings
⊗Rice Starch
⊗Rice Syrup (barley enzymes)
☑Rice Vinegar (check all ingredients, safe if distilled)
☑Ricinoleic Acid

⊗ Risotto (Italian rice, see page 24)

☑ Romano Bean (chickpea)

⊗ Roquefort Cheese (listed as safe on most lists but usually contains trace amounts of gluten)

☑ Rosematta

☑ Rosin

⊗ Rough Rice

⊗ Roux (thickener, usually wheat flour)

☑ Royal Jelly

⊗ Rusk

⊗ Rye

☑ Saccharin

☑ Safflower Oil (many Celiacs have reactions)

☑ Saffron

☑ Sago

☑ Sago Flour or Starch

☑ Sago Palm

☑ Saifun (bean threads)

☑ Salba

☑ Salt

☑ Saponin

? Sausage (check for fillers)

? Seasonings (caution with vague terms)

☑ Seaweed (plain dry versions safe; caution with snack versions with added flavors like soy, which is unsafe)

⊗ Secalin

⊗ Seitan

⊗ Semolina

⊗ Semolina Triticum

☑ Sesame

☑ Sesame Butter (pure)

☑ Shea

☑ Sherry Vinegar

⊗Shortening (can contain vitamin E from wheat germ)

⊗Shot Wheat (triticum aestivum)

⊗Shoyu

☑Silicon Dioxide

⊗Sirimi (binder: usually wheat or cornstarch)

⊗Small Spelt

☑Soba (verify it is 100% buckwheat; also high risk of cross contamination)

☑Sodium Acetate

☑Sodium Acid Pyrophosphate

☑Sodium Alginate

☑Sodium Ascorbate

☑Sodium Benzoate

? Sodium Caseinate (contains MSG)

☑Sodium Citrate

☑Sodium Erythrobate

☑Sodium Hexametaphosphate

☑Sodium Lactate

☑Sodium Lauryl Sulfate (gluten free, but harmful product found in synthetic soap, shampoo, detergents – try to replace with phosphate free, natural products)

☑Sodium Metabisulphite

☑Sodium Nitrate

☑Sodium Phosphate

☑Sodium Polyphosphate

☑Sodium Silaco Aluminate

? Sodium Starch Glycolate (may be from any starch)

☑Sodium Stearoyl Lactylate

☑Sodium Sulphite

☑Sodium Stannate

☑Sodium Tripolyphosphate

⊗Soft Wheat
☑Sorbic Acid
☑Sorbitan Monostearate
☑Sorbitan Trioleate
☑Sorbitan Tristearate
☑Sorbitol-Mannitol (can cause IBS symptoms)
⊗Sorghum (see page 24)
⊗Sorgum (see page 24)
☑Soy (many Celiacs sensitive; soy sauce unsafe)
☑Soya Flour
☑Soya Starch
☑Soybean
☑Soy Lecithin
☑Soy Milk (check for added flavors or malt)
☑Soy Protein
☑Soy Protein Isolate
⊗Soy Sauce
⊗Spelt (triticum spelta)
☑Sphingolipids Soba (if it is 100% buckwheat)
?Spices (verify for fillers)
?Spirits (see alcohol)
⊗Sprouted Wheat or Barley
?Stabilizers (verify source)
?Starch (can be made from many sources)
⊗Stativa
☑Stearamide
☑Stearamine
☑Stearates
☑Stearic Acid
☑Stearyl Citrate
⊗Stearyldimoniumhydroxypropyl Hydrolyzed Wheat
Protein

☑Stearyl Lactate
☑Stevia
⊗Stilton Cheese
⊗Stock Cubes
⊗Strong Flour
⊗Stout
☑Streptococcus Thermophilus
☑Subflower Seed
☑Succinic Anhydride
⊗Succotash (corn and beans)
☑Sucralose
☑Sucrose
☑Suet, raw fat safe (dried packet suet unsafe)
☑Sugar (pure form, caution with powdered sugar)
☑Sulfites
☑Sulfosuccinate
☑Sulfur Dioxide
☑Sulphuric Acid
☑Sulphurous Acid
☑Sunflower oil or seed
⊗Surimi
☑Sweet Chestnut Flour
☑Sweet Potato
⊗Sweet Rice Flour
☑Tagatose
☑Tahini (100% pure sesame)
☑Tallow
⊗Tamari
☑Tamarind
☑Tannic Acid
☑Tapioca
☑Tapioca Flour

☑Tapioca Starch
☑Tara Gum
☑Taro
☑Tarro
☑Tarrow Root
☑Tartaric Acid
☑Tartrazine (gluten free, but harmful to health)
☑TBHQ - tertiary butylhydroquinone (gluten free preservative, but shown to be toxic in studies)
☑Tea (check for added ingredients)
☑Tea-Tree Oil
☑Teff (cross contamination risk)
?Tempeh (often contains soy sauce)
☑Tepary Bean
⊗Teriyaki Sauce
⊗Texmati Rice (see page 24)
?Textured Vegetable Protein (wheat or soy)
☑Thaumatin
☑Thiamine Hydrochloride
☑Thiamine Mononitrate
⊗Timopheevi Wheat (triticum timopheevii)
☑Titanium Dioxide
☑Tocopherols
☑Tofu (check for added ingredients)
☑Tolu Balsam
⊗Tortillas
☑Torula Yeast
⊗Tostada
☑Tragacanth
☑Tragacanth Gum
☑Triacetin

☑Tributyrin

☑Tricalcium Phosphate

☑Triethyl Citrate

⊗Triticale X Triticosecale

⊗Triticum Vulgare (wheat) Germ Extract or Oil

☑Trypsin

☑Turmeric

?TVP (can be wheat or soy)

☑Tyrosine

⊗Udon (usually wheat or corn)

⊗Unbleached Flour

☑Urad/Urid Beans

☑Urad/Urid Dal (peas) Vegetables

☑Urad/Urid flour

☑Urd

⊗Valencia Rice (see page 24)

☑Vanilla Extract (pure vanilla)

☑Vanilla Flavoring (verify it is pure vanilla)

☑Vanillin

⊗Vavilovi Wheat (triticum aestivum)

?Vegetable Broth

?Vegetable Gum (verify grains)

?Vegetable Protein

⊗Vegetable shortening

⊗Vegetable Starch (verify contents)

?Vinegar (apple cider, wine, or balsamic are usually safe; highly varied processes in making vinegar, manufacturer must be contacted in each case despite most lists claiming distilled as safe - additives are often added after distillation process. very inexpensive white vinegar must be verified)

⊗Vital Wheat Gluten

⊗Vulgar

⊗Waxy Maize

⊗Wehani Rice (see page 24)

⊗Wheat, abyssinian hard triticum durum

⊗Wheat Amino Acids

⊗Wheat Bran

⊗Wheat Bran Extract

⊗Wheat Bulgur

⊗Wheat Durum Triticum

⊗Wheat Germ

⊗Wheat Germamidopropyldimonium Hydroxypropyl

⊗Wheat Germ Glycerides

⊗Wheat Germ Oil

☑Wheatgrass (grass portion is safe, the seeds are not; if cutting to juice, cut one cm away from seed)

⊗Wheat Nuts

⊗Wheat Protein

⊗Wheat Triticum Aestivum

⊗Wheat Triticum Monococcum

☑Whey (pure whey safe; modified versions may contain trace amounts of gluten)

☑Whey Protein Concentrate

☑Whey Protein Isolate

⊗White Grain Vinegar

⊗Whole-Meal Flour

⊗Whole Wheat Berries

⊗Whole Wheat Flour

⊗Wild Einkorn (triticum boeotictim)

⊗Wild Emmer (triticum dicoccoides)

⊗Wild Rice (see page 24)

☑Wine (standard wine is safe; wine coolers are not)

☑Wine Vinegar (safe, see vinegar)

☑Wood Smoke

⊗Worcestershire (usually contains barley)

☑Xanthophyll

?Xanthum Gum (can be made from wheat, soy, corn, or dairy)

☑Xylanase

☑Xylitol

☑Yam

☑Yam Flour

?Yeast (Autolyzed, Baker's, Nutritional, Torula safe; Brewer's not safe. often grown or dried on wheat flour, side with caution, buy specially marked GF versions)

☑Yogurt (caution with added flavors, fruit, toppings; added muesli or granola unsafe)

⊗Zein (see page 24)

☑Zinc Oxide

☑Zinc Sulfate

WE, THE CONSUMER

Please look out for petitions you can sign, or letters you can send to government to bring transparency to food labels. As consumers, we have a right to know what is in our food, including genetically modified foods.

These dangerous laws must be changed, and like all social change, it is only through pressure from the public that it can happen.

As consumers, we don't realize we are collectively the most powerful force in the world – on ALL issues, food and otherwise. With every dollar we spend, we create demand, which dictates supply. By being aware of our choices and buying accordingly, we can create change. Every dollar spent is a powerful vote.

notes

notes

notes

notes

notes

notes

notes

notes

notes

notes

notes

notes

notes

notes

notes

notes

notes

ESSENTIAL BASICS PAGE INDEX

ARTIFICIAL FLAVOR/COLOR 11
CANDY, CHOCOLATE, COUGH DROPS 11
CHEESE 11
COLAS & COMMON DRINKS 11
CROSS CONTAMINATION 12
DETOX & DIETS 13
GLUTEN vs. WHEAT 13
GRAS 13
GROCERY GUIDES 13
GROUND SPICE 14
KITCHEN CARE 14
MEDICATION 15
MINDSET 15
MODIFIED INGREDIENTS 15
NATURAL FLAVOR/COLOR 15
NON-FOOD ITEMS 15
RAW FOOD 15
SAFE FOODS 16
SUSHI 16
TEA 16
THE LAW 16
VINEGAR 16
VITAMIN DEFICIENCIES 17
VITAMINS & SUPPLEMENTS 17

ALL GRAINS 24

PRINTED IN THE UNITED STATES

LIBRARY AND ARCHIVES CANADA

KARR, JAQUI.

GLUTEN SAFE & UNSAFE INGREDIENT LIST: THE FUNDAMENTAL POCKET GUIDE FOR CELIACS

ISBN: 978-0-9813198-8-9

3RD REVISION

Made in the USA
Lexington, KY
21 January 2012